Contents

Savoury

Breads

Sweets & Treats

Savoury

Baked Salmon

Ingredients serves 1

1 fillet of salmon

30 grams butter

1 tsp fresh finely chopped chives

1 tsp fresh chopped parsley

1/4 fresh chilli pepper, sliced

10 grams chopped broccoli

10 grams green beans

5 grams spinach

1 garlic clove, crushed inside skins

1 drop of olive oil

1 slice of lime

Directions

1. Pre-heat an oven to 220°C / 200°C fan.
2. On a sheet of baking parchment or tin foil, pour the drop of oil into the centre.
3. Lay the green beans, broccoli, and spinach on the sheet. Then place the salmon on top.
4. Place the butter, chives, parsley, garlic clove and chilli.
5. Lay the slice of lime on top, now wrap the salmon inside the sheet, making sure to create a bag, leaving room for the fish and veg to steam inside.
6. Place in the oven and cook for 15-20mins or until cooked to your liking.

Beef and Mushroom Stew

Ingredients serves 2

Stew

350 grams Beef Shin

80 grams Smoked Bacon Lardons

3 Carrots, roughly chopped

80 grams Porcini mushrooms

500 ml Red Wine

500 ml Beef Stock

3 whole Shallots

3 grams fresh parsley, left on the stalk

2 tbsp seasoned plain flour

1 tbsp Olive oil

Herby Dumplings

3 1/2 tbsp Suet

5 tbsp plain flour

1/2 tbsp tarragon

1/2 tbsp sage

1/2 tbsp dried parsley

1/2 tbsp dried chives

water to bind

Directions

1. Gently heat the wine until hot but not bubbling.
2. Pre-heat the oven to 170°C /150°C fan.
3. Soak the porcini, fresh parsley and the shallots in the wine. Removing from heat.
4. Heat and oven proof casserole dish on the hob. Dry fry the bacon lardons until starting to brown. Then add the shallots from the wine and brown,then remove.
5. Add the olive oil to heat. Coat the beef shin in the seasoned flour and the brown in the pot. Once browned remove.
6. Boil a little bit of water and tip in the pot to de-glaze. Add the red wine that the mushrooms have been soaking in, but do not add the mushrooms. Cook for about 2-3mins on high.
7. Add the carrots, followed by the meat, shallots and mushrooms. Take the fresh parsley, chop up and add.
8. Add the beef stock, keep on the heat until it begins to bubble.
9. Place the lid on and place in the oven for 2.5hours. Then add the dumplings.
10. For the dumplings: mix all the ingredients with water until it binds in to a firm but wet mixture. Shape and place in the pot with the lid on, raising the oven temp to 190°C / 170°C fan. Cook for 20mins. Remove the lid and cook for 5-10 more mins.

Beef Hotpot

Ingredients

500 ml Beef stock

1 large carrot chopped

2 baby turnips, chopped

1 shallot, finely diced

4 clove of garlic, crushed and finely diced

1 tbsp smooth salsa

2 potatoes, sliced in to thin pieces

25 grams butter, melted

1/2 tbsp dried parsley

250 grams Braising Steak, cut into cubes

Directions

1. Pre-heat an oven to 190°C / 170°C fan.

2. Heat 1 tbsp of veg oil in a hob and oven safe pot. Brown the meat.

3. Add the shallot, garlic and salsa and cook for 2mins.

4. Mix in the carrot and turnips, pour in the stock and de-glaze the pot. bring to boil.

5. put the lid on the pot and place in the oven for 1h30mins.

6. note : Boil some water and top up liquid if needed.

7. place the potato slices on top, mix the parsley and butter and brush the butter over the potatoes. Return to the oven without the lid for 30mins or until crispy on top.

8. serve

Braised Lamb Shank

Ingredients serves 1

1 lamb shank

4 shallots, peeled whole

3 clove of garlic, crushed

25 grams dried porcini mushrooms, soaked in 250ml of boiling water for 25mins

1 tbsp double concentrate tomato purée

500 ml chicken stock

1 carrot, roughly chopped

1 tsp dried rosemary

2 tbsp olive oil

Directions

1. Separate the porcini from its stock, keeping the stock on one side, and chop.
2. Pre-heat an oven to 160°C / 140°C fan.
3. Heat the oil in an oven proof pot. Brown the lamb shank then put to one side.
4. Brown the shallots then add the garlic, carrots and mushrooms, cooking for a 2-3mins.
5. Use a little bit of chicken stock to de-glaze the pot.
6. Add the porcini stock and tomato purée.
7. Add the lamb shank back to the pot and add the chicken stock until its about 2/3rds covering the shank.
8. Add the rosemary, cover and cook for 3hours in the oven.
9. Remove the lid and cook for another 15-20mins.

Burgers

Ingredients serves 16

500 grams fresh Minced Beef

1 1/2 tbsp Tomato Purée

3 clove of Garlic, crushed

1 Onion, very finely diced

15 grams Spinach, chopped into small pieces

1 tbsp dried Basil

4 rounds of shop brought bread, blended into crumbs

Salt and Pepper to season

1 Egg, beaten (have another ready just in case)

Directions

1. Place the meat, purée, garlic, onion, bread crumbs, spinach, basil all together in a bowl.
2. Mix thoroughly.
3. Gradually add the egg until the mixture becomes a firm combined mixture.
4. Shape into burgers, place them on and cover with greaseproof paper, storing in the fridge to rest for a couple of hours, overnight better.
5. Cook when ready, or if meat was fresh you could freeze them.

Cheese Mushroom Baskets

Ingredients serves 2

100 grams filo pastry

80 grams smoke bacon lardons

140 grams exotic mushrooms

150 grams goats cheese

25 grams goats butter

20 grams butter, melted

2 shallots, finely diced

4 clove of garlic, crushed

1/2 grams finely chopped fresh parsley

3 grams chives, finely chopped

20 grams spinach

25 ml boiled water

Directions

1. Pre-heat an oven 190°C / 170°C fan.

2. Butter the under side of 2 dishes with some of the melted butter.

3. Layer some pastry over the dishes, buttering in between the layers. Cook in the oven for 12-15mins.

4. Dry fry the lardons in a pan on a high heat.

5. Reduce the heat and add the butter to melt.

6. Add the shallot and garlic and sweat down.

7. Add the mushrooms.

8. Add some boiled water to de-glaze the pan, then add the cheese to create the sauce.

9. Remove the pastry baskets and place on a plate. Layer some spinach on the bottom of each, then pour over the cheese and mushroom sauce.

Cheese Straws

200 grams Self Raising Flour

1 pinch Cayenne Pepper

125 grams Unsalted Butter

125 grams Parmesan (or vegetarian alternative)

2 Eggs

1 tsp Dijon Mustard

Sesame Seeds to sprinkle on top

Directions

1. Pre-Heat an oven to 190°c / 170°c fan.
2. Put the flour, pepper, and butter in a bowl and rub together to make breadcrumbs.
3. Add the cheese and mix in.
4. Crack one egg in to the bowl, then separate the other egg, placing the whites to one side and the yolk in the bowl. Add the mustard and mix together.
5. Once the mixture binds, knead for approx. 30secs. Wrap in cling film and rest in the fridge for a couple of hours.
6. Roll out to approx. 0.5 - 0.75mm thickness, slice into fingers, give them a gentle twist and place on a baking tray.
7. Beat the egg white and wash the fingers with it. Sprinkle over the sesame seeds and place in the oven for 18 - 20mins, until golden brown.
8. Once cooked, remove and allow to cool.

Chicken Curry

Ingredients serves 2

Paste

50 grams tomato purée

10 grams turmeric

15 grams garam masala

45 grams water

4 clove of garlic, crushed

1 tsp chives

salt and pepper for seasoning

Spices & Herbs mix

1 whole dried chilli

4 cardamom pods

5 black peppercorns

1 shard of cinnamon

1/2 tsp cumin seed

1 bay leaf

1 tsp basil

other ingredients

500 ml chicken stock

1 pepper, sliced

50 grams runner beans, sliced

50 grams spinach

375 grams (2 thighs) chicken thigh, boned and skinned

400 grams tinned chopped tomatoes

2 tbsp olive oil

Directions

1. to make the paste: Mix all the ingredients for the paste. This can be done in advance and chilled in the fridge before use.

2. Pre-heat the oven to 190°C / 170°C fan.

3. Heat the oil on the hob, in an oven proof pot. Add the spices and herbs and heat for 20-30 seconds.

4. Brown the chicken thighs.

5. Add the paste mix and cook for about 1-2mins.

6. Add the pepper and runner beans. Mix round well and add the tomatoes. Scrape the bottom of the pot and mix well.

7. Pour in the stock, scrape the bottom again and mix. Bring the chicken to sit near the top of the sauce, heat until it starts to bubble then place in the oven for 45mins.

8. Add the spinach and cook for a further 15mins.

9. serve

Crispy Chicken Wraps

Ingredients serves 4

crispy coating

2 tsp paprika

1 tsp ground cumin

1/2 tsp cayenne pepper

1/2 tsp ground coriander

1 tsp garlic granules

1 tsp mild chilli powder

80 grams breadcrumbs

other ingredients

2 tbsp vegetable oil

A handful of mixed leaves (spinach, rocket, watercress)

4 corn tortilla wraps

2 chicken breasts, cut into long thin strips

1 yellow pepper, cut into thin strips

1 red pepper, cut into thin strips

70 grams mild cheese, cut into equal sized strips

other items needed

1 strong medium to large food bag

tin foil

Directions

1. Preheat oven to 220°c / 200°c fan.

2. Mix all the spices together and then mix with the breadcrumbs.

3. Place the chicken in the food bag and add the oil and the coating mixture. Tie a knot in the bag to ensure completely sealed and shake until chicken is well coated.

4. Play the chicken strips onto a baking tray and cook in the oven for 18-20mins, or until cooked.

5. On the tortilla wraps, lay the mixed leaves, peppers and cheese. Once the chicken is done, reduce the heat to 200°c / 180°c fan, and lay the chicken strips onto the wraps.

6. Roll up the wraps and then cover with tin foil. Place in the oven for 10mins. (leave longer for a crispier wrap)

Exotic Mushroom Pasta

Ingredients serves 2

main

125 grams Oyster Mushrooms
140 grams Mixed Exotic Mushrooms
1 Red Bell Pepper, sliced into strips
1 Lemon, cut in half
50 grams Butter, cut into cubes
30 grams finely grated Parmesan (or vegetarian alternative)
2 tbsp dried Parsley
3 clove of Garlic, crushed
3 tbsp Olive Oil
1 pinch Salt

pasta

300 grams Flour (00 or plain will do)
3 medium Eggs
1 tbsp Olive Oil
1 pinch Salt

Directions

1. Sieve the flour into a bowl. Using your hand, create a well in the middle.

2. Crack the 3 eggs into the well.

3. Add 1tbsp of olive oil and a pinch of salt.

4. Gradually pull the flour into the eggs, using your hands to mix them together, revolving your hand in a claw shape and then bringing the flour over and pressing in.

5. Once mixed, knead the dough thoroughly until it's smooth and elastic. Wrap it in cling film and place in the fridge for 30mins.

6. Remove the dough from the fridge and place onto well floured surface. Roll the dough out into a long sheet of pasta. Whilst rolling out, gently pull on one of the sides to help stretch it out. Ensure you continually turn the pasta dough around and flip it over on the other side as you go.

7. Once rolled to about 3mm thickness (if you hold it up to the light you should be able to see your hand through it), finely slice the pasta into long thin strips.

8. Bring a pan of salted water to boil.

9. Heat 3tbsp of olive oil in a large deep frying pan.

10. Add the pepper and crushed garlic with a pinch of salt, frying gently until the garlic is browned.

11. Add the mushrooms to the frying pan and add the pasta to the boiling water. Cook both for about 3-5mins.

12. Squeeze hall the lemon into the frying pan and reduce the heat to low.

13. Using tongs or a slotted spoon, take the pasta out of the water and add to the frying. Allow any of the water to drip from the pasta into the frying pan. DO NOT DRAIN.

14. Squeeze the other half of the lemon, stir around then add the parsley, butter and cheese.

15. Keep mixing until the cheese and butter have melted and the pasta has a nice sheen from the sauce coating it.

Fish Pie

Ingredients serves 1

Filling

160 grams Salmon

150 grams Haddock

60 grams Raw King Prawns

2 Shallots, whole

3 clove of Garlic, crushed in skin

35 grams Butter

35 grams Plain Flour

300 ml Milk

1 tbsp Fresh Flat Leaf Parsley, chopped

Topping

35 grams Butter

100 ml Milk

500 grams Potatoes, peeled add cut into chunks

Directions

1. Boil a pan of seasoned water, and add the potatoes. Boil for about 10mins.
2. Place the shallots, garlic, salmon, haddock and milk into a frying pan. Heat till just about boiling then reduce the heat and simmer for about 8-10mins.
3. Remove the fish and leave to one side and pour the milk into a jug.
4. Drain the potatoes, and put back into the pan, adding the butter on top.
5. In a fresh pan, gently heat butter until totally melted. Increase heat, add the flour and beat with a whisk, keeping on the heat.
6. Pour in the pouching milk, whisking as you do, add the parsley and simmer on a low heat for about 5mins. Make sure to continuously whisking the mixture with your whisk.
7. Begin mashing the potatoes, adding the milk as you go. Make sure you get it to a nice smooth consistency. Season to taste.
8. Pre-heat an oven to 190°C / 170°C fan.
9. Flake the fish and add it to a dish along with the raw prawns. Fold in the sauce, making sure all the fish is well covered.
10. Spoon over the mash on the top. Smooth it out and then use the back of a fork to decorate the top.
11. Put the pie in the oven for 30-35mins.

Hare Ragu

Ingredients

450 grams saddle of hare

400 grams tinned chopped tomatoes

1 chicken stock cube, mixed with 100ml of boiled water

2 tbsp double concentrate tomato purée

1 parsnip, use a peeler to cut in to ribbons

2 carrots, use a peeler to cut into ribbons

100 ml red wine

2 tbsp olive oil

140 grams pappardelle pasta

Directions

1. Heat the oil in a wok on a high heat.

2. Brown the meat in the wok. Once browned, remove and put to one side.

3. Add the parsnip and carrots and cook for 1-2 mins.

4. Pour in the wine and de-glaze the wok. Reduce the wine by about 1/2.

5. Add the tomato purée and tinned tomatoes and stir in.

6. Add the hare back to the wok and add the stock.

7. Cover the wok and reduce heat to simmer for about 1hour.

8. Remove the hare to rest. Raise the heat to high and part cover. Make sure you keep stirring to ensure nothing sits and burns at the bottom of the wok.

9. Boil some water and cook the pasta. Drain the pasta before it is completely cooked.

10. Cut the hare in the chunks and add back to the wok along with the pasta and mix well to ensure everything is well covered. Cook for about 2-3 mins on a low heat.

11. Serve with some grated parmesan.

Lamb Jamaican Jerk

Ingredients

1 lamb shank

1 tbsp Jamaican jerk seasoning

2 tbsp vegetable oil

400 grams tinned chopped tomatoes

1 lamb stock cube, mixed in 400ml of boiled water

1 pepper, chopped

1 chilli pepper, chopped

3 clove of garlic, crushed

4 shallots, chopped

1 lemon, halved

1 sweet potato, chopped

60 grams basmati and wild rice

Directions

1. Create a marinade using the oil and seasoning. Cover the meat and leave to stand for at least 15mins.

2. Pre-heat an oven to 170°C / 150°C fan.

3. In a heat proof pot, brown the meat. Once browned remove and rest.

4. Add any excess marinade to the pot and brown the shallots. Then add the garlic, stir in and cook for 1-2 mins.

5. Add the pepper and chilli, cooking for 1-2mins, the squeeze in lemon juice to de-glaze the pan (use both halves of the lemon).

6. Add the tomatoes and stock to the pot, mix and then place the meat back to the pot. Bring the liquid to a bubble, place on the lid and place in the oven for 2hours.

7. At this stage, add the sweet potato and place back in the oven for 1hour.

8. With about 30mins to go, remove the lid from the pot, placing back in the oven and begin to prep the rice. Place in a pan of boiling water and cook for about 25mins, or until you are happy the rice is cooked to your taste.

Lasagne

Ingredients serves 2

Pasta

300 grams flour (00 or plain)

3 medium eggs, yolks and whites separated

5 tbsp olive oil

salt and pepper to season

additional flour for the surface

Ragu

1 tbsp olive oil

1 pepper, diced

400 grams tinned chopped tomatoes

400 grams braising steak

3 clove of garlic, crushed

25 grams butter

6 basil leaves, thinly sliced

150 ml red wine

2 finely diced shallots

Béchamel Sauce

250 ml milk

1 onion, halved

2 clove of garlic, crushed in skin

20 grams plain flour

20 grams butter

70 grams goats cheese

1 bouquet garni

Lasagne

70 grams mild cheddar cheese

1. For the ragu: Heat the olive oil in a pot and brown the braising steak. Remove the meat and reduce the heat to low. Add the butter and gently heat until melted. Once melted, add the garlic and shallots and garlic, and sweat down for 2-3mins. Add the pepper for 1-2mins then pour in the wine, scraping the bottom of the pot to de-glaze. Cook for 2-3mins then stir in the tomatoes, re-add the meat and cover, simmering for 90mins, ensuring you stir throughout.

2. Now for the bechamel: Pour the milk into a pan. Add the onion, garlic and bouquet garni. Bring to boil then remove from the heat. Leave to one side for 1 hour.

3. For the pasta: Place the flour into a bowl, create a well, pour in the egg yolks, olive oil and seasoning. Mix together adding the whites as you go until it binds together. Flour a work surface, tip out the dough and knead until the dough becomes smooth and elasticy. Wrap in cling film and chill in the fridge for 30mins. Roll out the dough on a work surface until it is about 2-3mm in thickness (you can test this by holding your hand behind to see if you can see it), then cut to the size desired.

4. Continue the ragu: Remove the lid from the pot, give it a stir and add in the basil, seasoning and then simmer for another 30mins.

5. Continue the pasta: In a pan, boil some seasoned water, put the pasta into the pan and cook for 3-4mins, then remove and place to one side.

6. Continue the béchamel: Pour the milk into a jug, removing the onion and garlic. Gently heat the butter in a pan then stir in the flour using a whisk for 2-3mins. Pour in the milk, whisking as you do. Bring to boil, reduce the heat and add the goats cheese. Simmer for 10mins, storing regularly.

7. To make the Lasagne: Pre-heat and oven to 220°C/200°C fan. In a tray, layer up the lasagne as follows: pasta, bechamel, ragu, pasta, bechamel,

Meatball Wraps

Ingredients *serves 2*

Meatballs

400 grams Sausages, skin removed

250 grams Pork mince

1 tbsp Flat Leaf Parsley, finely chopped

70 grams Seasoned Plain Flour

Flat Bread

250 grams Seasoned Plain Flour

1 cup of water

Main

25 grams Butter

1 tbsp Olive Oil

2 tbsp Double Concentrate Tomato Purée

400 grams Tinned Chopped Tomatoes

2 Shallots, finely diced

2 clove of Garlic, crushed

1 Pepper, diced

3 Basil leaves, roughly chopped

12 slice of Pepperoni

1/2 Chilli Pepper, sliced finely

70 grams Grated Mild Cheddar Cheese

Directions

1. For the Meatballs: In a bowl, mix the pork mince, sausage meat and parsley, mashing with the back of a fork to help tenderise the mince. Take approximately 1/2tbsp of the mixture and shape into a ball. Roll this in the flour and set to one side. You should be able to get approximately 20 meatballs. Select how many you want to serve per person (6 works well) and freeze the rest. Place the meatballs you wish to use in the fridge to chill for 30mins.

2. For the flat bread: Slowly pour the water into the flour and mix in. Keep doing this until you have bonded it into a good dough. Flour a surface and place the dough onto the surface. Knead well until you create a nice smooth elasticy dough. Heat a dry pan on high. Roll out the dough until really thin. Cut out to the size of a plate and dry fry in the pan. Put to one side to cool and make as many wraps as you need. The mixture can make at least 6, depending on plate size.

3. Heat the oil in a heat proof dish and brown the meatballs.

4. Reduce the hear to low, remove the meatballs and add the butter to gently heat.

5. Add the garlic and shallots and sweat down for 2-3mins.

6. Add the pepper and chilli and cook for a further 2mins.

7. Stir in the purée, then add the pepperoni.

8. Stir in the tinned tomatoes, heat the sauce till bubbling. Reduce the heat to simmer and add the basil.

9. Add back the meatballs and cook for 35-40mins.

10. Spoon some of the meatballs on to a wrap making sure you put one slice of pepperoni per meatball.

11. Pre-heat an oven to 190°C / 170°C fan.

12. Spoon over a bit more sauce, sprinkle on some cheese, the roll and wrap up tight. Then wrap this inside some tin foil, put to one side and repeat for as many wraps as you are making. Freeze any excess sauce, this can be used in another dish, maybe even with your meatballs. Remember to mark not vegetarian friendly if that could be an issue.

13. Cook in the oven for about 15-20mins.

Mild Vegetable Curry

Ingredients serves 2

Spices

1 Dried whole Chilli

4 Cardamom pods

5 Black Pepper Corns

1/2 tsp ground Mace

1/2 grams shard of Cinnamon

Paste (mix all together)

3 tbsp Double concentrate tomato purée

4 clove of garlic, crushed

1 tbsp water

1 tbsp Turmeric

1/2 tbsp Garam Massala

other ingredients

400 ml Coconut milk

100 ml Vegetable stock

2 tbsp Olive oil

2 Potatoes, peeled and chopped into chunks

120 grams wild Mushrooms

1/2 Courgette, peeled and chopped into chunks

50 grams Spinach

Directions

1. Heat the oil in a pan and add the spices. Cook for around 20-30seconds.

2. Add the courgette and potato chunks and brown off for 2-3mins.

3. Add the paste and cook for 2mins. Make sure to cover all the veg.

4. Pour in the stock and de-glaze. Follow this by adding the coconut milk.

5. Put the lid on and simmer on a low heat until potatoes start to soften. Make sure to occasionally stir.

6. Add the mushrooms and cook until the potatoes are fully cooked.

7. Turn off the heat and stir in the spinach for 5mins.

8. Serve

Mixed Game Terrine

Ingredients

terrine

400 grams mixed game, diced into chunks roughly

1 tbsp fresh chive, finely diced

12 pieces of streaky bacon

10 grams spinach, finely sliced/shredded (add more if you want)

2 clove of garlic, crushed and finely diced up

7 regular sausages, remove from skins

jam

200 ml water

100 grams caster sugar

2 bramley apples, peeled and cut roughly

1 granny smith apple, peeled and cut roughly

3 pears, peeled and cut roughly

Directions

1. Pre-heat an oven to 220°c / 200°c fan.

2. Line a terrine or bread tin with the bacon, make sure the bacon overlaps the tins sides.

3. In a bowl, mix together the sausage meat, chives, garlic and spinach with some salt and pepper for seasoning.

4. Add a layer of the sausage mix on top of the bacon.

5. Brown the mixed game in a pan. Add a layer of game on top of the sausage mix.

6. Add a second layer of the sausage mix, followed by a second layer of game. Repeat as many times as necessary, ensuring you finish with a layer of sausage mix.

7. Wrap the bacon around and then cover with tin foil.

8. Place in the oven for 1-1h30mins or until cooked. Make sure the core temperature reaches at least 73°c for a minute or two.

9. Leave to cool in the tray, with a second tray pressing and weighted down on top of the meat. (separate the two trays with baking parchment)

10. Tip out excess juices created, then remove the meat, wrap in cling film and store in the fridge overnight.

11. For the jam, add all the jam ingredients into a pan and bring to boil. Reduce the heat to low and cook for about 1 hour, until most of the apple is broken down. Use your spoon to stir and break up the fruit as you go.

12. Pour into a jam jar and allow to cool with lid off, then place in fridge.

Moroccan Chicken Cous Cous

Ingredients serves 2

Aubergine Paste (this can be made in advance and chilled)

1 Aubergine

4 clove of garlic, crushed

1 tbsp olive oil

1 tbsp turmeric

salt and pepper for seasoning

Main dish

Aubergine paste (see above)

2 chicken drumsticks

2 chicken thighs

2 tbsp olive oil, 1 in a heat proof pot and the other in a food bag.

400 grams tinned chopped tomatoes

1 pepper, sliced

125 grams cous cous

500 ml chicken stock

Main dish (Spices)

1 whole chilli pepper

1/2 grams cinnamon shard

1 tsp paprika

1 tsp Cumin

Directions

1. For the paste : pre-heat the oven to 190°C / 170°C fan. Pierce the outer skin of the aubergine, place in the oven and bake for 40-50mins. Once removed from the oven, open up and scoop out the insides and mush up. Add the rest of the paste ingredients and mix together. You can store this in the fridge and use later or use straight away.

2. Place the chicken in the food bag, add some salt and pepper, seal the bag and toss the chicken to cover in the oil.

3. Heat the oil in the pot. Add the spices for 20seconds.

4. Add the chicken and lightly brown. Once browned remove.

5. Add the pepper and cook for 1min.

6. Add the paste and cook for 1min.

7. Add the tomatoes and cook for 2mins.

8. Add the stock, scraping the bottom of the pot to de-glaze.

9. Place the chicken on top, skin down. Place the lid on the pot and cook on a low to medium heat for 35-40mins.

10. Once the chicken is cooked, remove the chicken to rest and ladle out 200ml of the stock in to a bowl or jug.

11. Add the cous cous to the separated stock, and leave to soak, fluffing up and separating with a fork after a couple mins.

12. Turn the heat up on the pot with remaining stock to a high setting and reduce for 5mins.

13. serve

Mushroom Cream Cheese, Garlic and Herb Crostinis

Ingredients serves 2

125 grams Exotic Mushrooms (larger ones chopped, smaller ones left whole)

2 clove of Garlic, crushed

2 tbsp Cream Cheese (heaped tbsp)

15 grams Fresh Flat Leaf Parsley, finely chopped

1 tbsp Olive Oil

salt and pepper to season

6 diagonally sliced pieces of French Bread

Directions

1. Heat the oil in a pan.
2. Put the bread onto the grill to toast.
3. Add the garlic and mushrooms together and fry gently until the mushrooms are soft.
4. Add the cream cheese and cook gently until the cheese becomes like a sauce.
5. Add the parsley and season to taste.

Mushroom Soup

serves 2

25 grams dried porcini mushrooms

500 ml vegetable stock

60 grams exotic mushrooms

2 shallots, diced finely

3 garlic cloves, crushed

1 tbsp double concentrate tomato purée

1 carrot, use a peeler to peel into ribbons

25 grams butter

1 grams fresh coriander, finely chopped

Directions

1. Soak the porcini in 250ml of boiling water for 25mins. Then separate the stock and mushrooms. Keep the stock and chop the porcini.

2. Melt the butter in a pan on a medium to low heat.

3. Add the shallots, garlic and carrots to the pan and cook gently for 2-3mins.

4. Add the coriander and all the mushrooms, cooking for another 2-3mins.

5. Use a little bit of the vegetable stock to de-glaze the pan. Then add in the porcini stock, tomato purée and vegetable stock. Season then bring up heat until the liquid begins to bubble.

6. Cook for about 30-35mins on a low heat.

Oxtail Soup

650 grams oxtail

1 beef stock gel

1 tbsp tomato purée

1 onion, roughly chopped

1 turnip, roughly chopped

1 carrot, roughly chopped

3 vine tomatoes, de-seeded and roughly chopped

850 ml boiled water

Directions

1. pre-heat the oven to 190°c / 170°c fan.

2. in an oven proof pot, heat 2tbsp of veg oil, brown the oxtail.

3. remove the oxtail. in the pot brown the onion, then add all the veg and purée. add salt and pepper to season.

4. with some of the boiled water, de-glaze the pot. add back the meat and pour in enough water to cover everything.

5. bring to boil and then put in the oven for 1hour.

6. stir the broth and then add the stock gel. return to the oven for 1.5hours. remember to check and top up water if needed, but allow reduction to half of where you started.

7. remove the pot from the oven

8. remove the meat from the pot. remove the meat of the bone and put in a food processor. add all the veg to the processor and some of the liquid. add some salt and pepper to taste.

9. blend the ingredients, add some more of the liquid and repeat. continue until all the cooking liquid is used.

10. at this stage you can freeze this safely for up to a month if you wish.

11. to serve - pour into a saucepan and heat gently till piping hot, do not boil. serve.

Pasta Meatball Bake

Ingredients *serves 2*

30 grams spinach
210 grams Fusilli Pasta (fresh or dry)
70 grams Mild Cheese, grated

Meatballs

400 grams Sausages, skin removed
250 grams Pork Mince
70 grams seasoned plain flour
1 tbsp Flat Leaf Parsley, finely chopped

Sauce

25 grams Butter
2 tbsp Double Concentrate Tomato Purée
400 grams Tinned Chopped Tomatoes
1 Pepper, sliced
2 Shallots, finely diced
2 clove of Garlic, crushed
3 Basil Leaves, roughly chopped
1/2 Chilli Pepper, sliced finely
1 tbsp olive oil

Directions

1. Pre heat an oven to 190°C / 170°C fan.

2. For the Meatballs: In a bowl, mix the pork mince, sausage meat and parsley, mashing with the back of a fork to help tenderise the mince. Take approximately 1/2tbsp of the mixture and shape into a ball. Roll this in the flour and set to one side. You should be able to get approximately 20 meatballs. Select how many you want to serve per person (6 works well) and freeze the rest. Place the meatballs you wish to use in the fridge to chill for 30mins.

3. For the sauce: Heat the oil in a heat proof dish and brown the meatballs. Reduce the hear to low, remove the meatballs and add the butter to gently heat. Add the garlic and shallots and sweat down for 2-3mins. Add the pepper and chilli and cook for a further 2mins. Stir in the purée. Stir in the tinned tomatoes, heat the sauce till bubbling. Reduce the heat to simmer and add the basil. Add back the meatballs and cook for 35-40mins.

4. Part cook the pasta in a pan of boiling water (the best thing to do is aim for 2/3rds of the cooking time). Drain out most of the water and leave to one side.

5. Remove the meatballs, take the sauce off the heat and add the spinach and pasta.

6. Pour the pasta into a suitable dish. Place the meatballs on top and cover in the cheese.

7. Place in the oven and cook until the cheese has melted.

8. Serve

Pizza

Ingredients

450 grams type 55 Flour or Bread Flour (super strong white bread flour works well)

330 ml Room Temperature Water

15 grams Dried Active Yeast

1 tsp Sugar

150 ml Warm Water (1 part boiling 2parts cold)

pizza dough 2nd stage

20 grams Ground Rock Salt

25 grams Caster Sugar

50 ml Olive Oil

120 grams type 55 or Bread Flour

toppings (make sure with the cheeses you use vegetarian friendly cheeses if it is for vegetarians)

125 grams Mozzarella Cheese, sliced

250 grams Mozzarella Cheese , sliced into fingers

200 grams parmesan Cheese (or vegetarian alternative)

3 tbsp Double Concentrate Tomato Purée (more if desired)

Add any toppings of your choice

Directions

1. In a 600ml (1 pint) jug, dissolve the sugar in the warm water.

2. Sprinkle in the yeast and whisk thoroughly.

3. Leave in a warm place until the surface is covered with approx. 2cm of froth (10-15mins).

4. Whisk again and use.

5. Put the flour in a bowl and add the yeast mixture.

6. Gradually add the room temperature water until you have a homogeneous, smooth dough.

7. Cover with cling film and leave to rise in a warm place for 8-12 hours.

8. On a lightly floured surface, punch the dough with one hand and fold with the other.

9. Use one hand to salt, sugar and olive oil a little at a time, swapping which you put in and when.

10. Finally add the flour.

11. Mix well and knead until the dough becomes elastic, has some body and slightly sticky.

12. Put in a clean bowl and cover with cling film, leaving for about 1 hour at room temperature.

13. Pre-heat an oven to 220°c / 200°c fan.

14. Roll the dough into a large circular base that will overlap the edges of your pizza tray by at least 3cm.

15. Place the mozzarella fingers around the edges and roll over to create a stuffed crust.

16. Spoon onto the base the tomato purée and using the spoon evenly spread it.

17. Place all your other ingredients on top, inc. the cheeses as you go.

18. Place in the oven for about 15-20mins or until golden brown and cooked through.

Pulled Pork

Ingredients

2 beef tomatoes, roughly chopped

2 red peppers, roughly chopped

4 clove of garlic, crushed in skin

3 shallots, roughly chopped

1 carrot, roughly chopped

1/2 chilli pepper

1 1/4 kg boneless pork shoulder

500 ml chicken stock

Directions

1. Pre-heat an oven to 190°C / 170°C fan.
2. Place all the veg into a deep roasting tin and drizzle with oil. Place in the oven to roast for 25-30mins.
3. Heat some oil in a frying pan and brown the pork shoulder.
4. Take the roasting tin out the oven and reduce the oven heat to 150°C / 130°C fan and place the pork on top of veg. Use a bit of the vegetable stock to deglaze the pan. Pour into the tin and then pour in the rest of the stock, make sure not to cover the meat completely.
5. Cover the tin with foil and place in the oven for about 5 hours.
6. Uncover the tin and cook for a further 25-30mins.
7. Once cooked, leave the pork to one side to rest. Place all the vegetables in a blender and blend to create a sauce. (Add some stock if you wish to thin it out)
8. Pull the meat apart using two forks. At this stage you can either mix in the meat with the sauce or use the sauce separately.
9. Warm up some pitta bread to serve.

Rabbit Casserole

Ingredients serves 4

main casserole

1 whole Rabbit, cut into decent size pieces. Chop the kidneys if you have them)

1 large onion, diced

2 clove of garlic, crushed

2 bramley apples, cut into chunks

50 grams plain flour (inside a food bag)

3 tbsp olive oil

900 ml vegetable stock

1 whole swede, cut into small pieces

3 carrots (roughly chopped)

2 parsnips, cut into small slices

1 handful of spinach leaves

dumplings

100 grams self raising flour

3 tbsp olive oil

2 tbsp dried mixed herbs

50 ml milk (be prepared you may need more)

salt and pepper

Directions

1. Pre-heat the oven to 170°c / 150°c fan oven.

2. Heat 3tbsp of olive oil in a large frying pan to a medium heat.

3. Place the rabbit in the food bag and shake to coat the meat in flour.

4. Take the meat out and place it in the frying pan to brown.

5. Once browned, remove and put to one side. Add the onion and garlic to the pan and cook on a low heat for 2-3 mins.

6. Add the carrots and the apple to the pan and cook for a further 2mins.

7. Tip the contents into a cast iron pot (or other oven friendly pot).

8. Add the rabbit.

9. Place the kidney in the frying pan and brown. Then pour in the stock and cook on a medium heat, allowing to bubble for 1-2 mins.

10. Tip the stock and kidneys into the pot and stir/mix all the contents together. Put the lid on the pot and place in the oven for 1 hour.

11. Put the swede and parsnip into the pot and return to cook for another 30mins.

12. Meanwhile, place the self raising flour in a bowl.

13. Pour in 3tbsp of olive oil, add the mixed herbs and abit of salt and pepper.

14. Gradually pour in the milk little by little until the mixture combines into a workable density. Firm but not soggy.

15. Place the dumplings in the pot, pressing down to cover them in the stock and cook with lid on for 25mins (or until a skewer can pierce and come out clean).

16. Remove the pot from the oven, add the spinach, stir in and stand for 5mins before serving.

Roast Duck, Black Pudding and Fondant Potatoes

Ingredients serves 2

for the duck

1 Duck Crown, approx. 900g

1 Baby Leek, sliced

2 slice of Lemon

8 Rashers of Smoky Bacon

A handful of Spinach leaves, stalks removed

for the fondant potatoes

500 ml Chicken Stock

3 clove of Garlic, crushed with skins on

100 grams Butter

1 tsp Rosemary

1 tsp Thyme

2 medium to large Potatoes, halved, peeled and shaped

for the gravy

2 tbsp Plain Flour

300 ml Chicken Stock

50 ml Red Wine

other

4 slice of Black Pudding

veg for accompaniment

Directions

1. Pre-Heat the oven to 200°C/180°C fan.

2. Season the Duck well and place on the spinach leaves to cover it.

3. Place the lemon slices on top of the spinach and sprinkle over leek evenly.

4. Place the bacon over the top, ensuring to cover completely. Place on a roasting tray and cook in the oven for approx. 1h - 1h10mins (or to your liking)

5. For the potatoes; heat the butter in a saucepan until foaming.

6. Add the potatoes for 4-5mins or until browned. Flip over and repeat cooking till browned.

7. Tip in the garlic and herbs followed by carefully pouring in the chicken stock. Pour in enough to cover 2/3rd's of the potatoes.

8. Place a lid over, reduce heat to low and braise for about 25-30mins or until very soft.

9. Check the cooking of the duck, 10mins before duck is removed from oven place the black pudding in to cook in the juices.

10. Remove the duck to rest for 10-15mins.

11. Remove black pudding, put aside and keep warm. Meanwhile, place the roasting pan on the hob and heat.

12. Add the flour and cook out collecting juices.

13. De-glaze using the red wine, then pour in the chicken stock, reducing to create the gravy.

14. serve with chosen veg.

Roasted Pigeon, Black Pudding, Fondant Potatoes and a Blackcurrant Sauce

Ingredients serves 2

2 whole pigeons

2 tbsp vegetable oil

100 ml chicken stock

3 clove of garlic, crushed

100 grams butter

1 tbsp dried parsley

100 grams black pudding

2 medium potatoes, peeled

1/2 tbsp caster sugar

150 grams blackcurrants

50 ml elderflower presse

100 ml Water

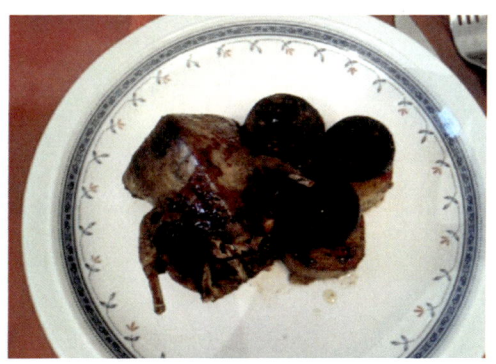

Directions

1. Pre-heat an oven to 220°c / 200°c fan.

2. Heat the oil in a frying pan and brown the pigeons.

3. Place the pigeons in a roasting tin and cover over with kitchen foil. Place in the oven for 50-60mins (or until cooked thoroughly).

4. Cut and shape the potatoes. Remove a section off each end, then cut into 2-3 pieces.

5. Heat the butter in a saucepan on medium heat until foaming.

6. Place the potatoes flat in the saucepan and leave to cook until browned (4-5mins approx.). Gently turn the potatoes and repeat on the other side.

7. Once browned, tip in the garlic and parsley and then gently pour in the chicken stock until it almost comes to the top of the potatoes and add some of the pigeon juices.

8. Put the lid on the saucepan and reduce heat to low and cook for 25-30mins until tender. During this time baste the potatoes by spooning over the stock juices every so often.

9. Place the caster sugar, blackcurrants, elderflower presse and water in the previously used frying pan. Bring to the boil on a medium heat.

10. Reduce the heat and allow to reduce until you have an almost syrupy like consistency.

11. Heat some oil in a frying pan and fry slices of black pudding.

12. Take the pigeon out the oven and rest for 5mins. Then serve.

Roasted Tomato and Pepper Soup

Ingredients serves 4

6 beef tomatoes (approx. 1.2kg)

2 red bell peppers

3 medium carrots

3 clove of garlic, skins on, crushed

300 ml vegetable stock

1/2 tbsp basil

olive oil for drizzling

Directions

1. Pre-heat an oven to 220°c / 200°c fan.
2. Chop all the veg roughly and tip onto a roasting tray.
3. Add the garlic and mix around. Season and drizzle olive oil over the veg and place in the oven for 20-25mins.
4. Remove the tray, mix around and cook for a further 15-20mins.
5. Place some of the veg in a blender and tip in the stock to blend. Gradually add the rest of the veg until it's all blended.
6. Add the basil. Allow to either cool and freeze or place in a saucepan and heat till piping hot.

Spinach Burgers

500 grams Spinach, tough stalks removed

2 Eggs, beaten

1 pinch freshly grated Nutmeg

3 clove of Garlic, crushed

100 grams fresh white Breadcrumbs

50 grams Parmesan, finely grated (or vegetarian alternative)

Directions

1. Blanch the spinach in a saucepan of boiling salted water for about 2 mins.
2. Remove, drain and allow to cool slightly.
3. Squeeze out as much water as you can and chop all the leaves finely.
4. Put the spinach in a bowl and stir in the egg, nutmeg, garlic, breadcrumbs and cheese, as well as some salt and pepper for seasoning.
5. Mix well until you reach a nice binding consistency. If the mixture is too wet, add some more breadcrumbs.
6. Shape into burgers, place on a sheet of greaseproof paper, another sheet on top of the burgers. Place in fridge to chill (overnight if possible), or freeze.

Wild Mushroom Rolls

280 grams mixed exotic mushrooms

250 grams oyster mushrooms

120 grams shitake mushrooms

1 medium onion, finely diced

2 clove of garlic, crushed

2 tsp ground coriander

1 tbsp dried parsley

40 grams butter

spinach leaves (amount required will vary based on leaf size)

640 grams puff pastry

1 large egg

Directions

1. Fry off the onion in a large pan on a low to medium heat.
2. Add the mushrooms and cook for 5mins.
3. Add the coriander, parsley and butter.
4. Season and place the mixture in a food processor and blend roughly.
5. Cut equally sized rectangles out of the puff pastry and lay the spinach on top of each piece.
6. Shape the mushroom mix into sausage shapes, place on the leaves and either wrap the spinach around or lay more on top.
7. Roll the pastry around and cut off excess. Repeat to create all rolls. At the stage they can be frozen.
8. Slice through the pastry to allow steam to escape, preventing soggy pastry.
9. Beat the egg and brush over the top of the rolls.
10. Cook at 200°c / 180°c fan for around 45mins or until golden brown.

Breads

50 – 50 Loaf

Ingredients

250 grams strong white flour

250 grams wholemeal flour

10 grams rock salt

10 grams active dry yeast

30 grams butter

350 ml water

olive oil

optional: seeds for topping

Directions

1. In a bowl add all the ingredients, keeping the yeast and salt apart. Combine all the ingredients with half of the water.
2. Continue to mix, gradually adding more water until fully combined.
3. Tip out onto a lightly oiled surface and knead for 10-15mins, until the dough becomes smooth.
4. Place the dough in a lightly oiled bowl and cover with cling film or tin foil and leave to prove for about 4hours.
5. Tip back out on a clean surface and knead for another 5mins.
6. Place the dough in a lined loaf tin. Place inside a plastic carrier to prove for another hour.
7. Pre-heat an oven to 220°C / 200°C fan.
8. Pour some boiled water into a baking tray and place at the bottom of your oven to create steam.
9. If you are going to top your loaf with seeds, do so now. Place the loaf in the oven for 15mins.
10. Reduce the heat to 190°C / 170°C fan and continue to bake for another 30mins or until fully baked. (You test this by tapping it, if it sounds hollow it should be done).
11. Leave on a wire rack to cool.

Bagels

Ingredients serves 8

150 grams Wholemeal bread flour

350 grams strong white bread flour

15 grams light muscavado sugar

10 grams rock salt

15 grams dried active yeast

4 tbsp olive oil

350 ml water

1 egg

Directions

1. Place all the dry ingredients and the oil into a bowl keeping the yeast away from the salt.
2. Pour in the water gradually until the dough begins to form. (You may not need it all)
3. Tip the dough onto a dry smooth surface and knead for 10mins.
4. Place the dough in a lightly oiled bowl and cover. Leave to prove for about 4hours.
5. Remove the dough and then knead for another 5mins.
6. Split into 8 equal sized balls, pierce the middle and swirl around your finger to create a ring shape. Place onto a baking tray lined with grease proof paper. (Make sure you leave room for the dough expanding, use a second tray if needed.)
7. Cover with a tea towel and prove for another 2hours.
8. Pre-heat an oven to 190°C / 170°C fan and bring a pan of water to boil.
9. One by one, boil each dough ring for 90s, turning over every 30s. Remove and place on a grease proof paper lined tray.
10. Crack the egg into a cup and beat with a fork. Use this to egg wash each bagel.
11. Place into the oven for 20-25mins or until golden brown.
12. Remove from the oven and allow to cool.

Bread Rolls

Ingredients serves 8

500 grams strong white flour

10 grams rock salt

10 grams active dry yeast

30 grams butter

350 ml water

olive oil

toasted sesame oil

Directions

1. In a bowl add all the ingredients, keeping the yeast and salt apart. Combine all the ingredients with half of the water.
2. Continue to mix, gradually adding more water until fully combined.
3. Tip out onto a lightly oiled surface and knead for 10-15mins, until the dough becomes smooth.
4. Place the dough in a lightly oiled bowl and cover with cling film or tin foil and leave to prove for about 4hours.
5. Tip back out on a clean surface and knead for another 5mins.
6. Split the dough into 8 equal sized portions. Cup your hand around the and move your hand in circular motion to form smooth dough balls. Place onto a lined baking tray. Make sure the rolls are evenly spaced.
7. Place inside a plastic carrier to prove for another hour.
8. Pre-heat an oven to 220°C / 200°C fan.
9. Pour some boiled water into a baking tray and place at the bottom of your oven to create steam.
10. Brush the sesame oil over the top of the rolls and place them in the oven for 15mins.
11. Reduce the heat to 190°C / 170°C fan and continue to bake for another 15mins or until fully baked. (You test this by tapping it, if it sounds hollow it should be done).
12. Leave on a wire rack to cool.

Chelsea Buns

Ingredients serves 10

for the dough

500 grams strong white flour

60 grams butter

10 grams dried active yeast

10 grams salt

10 grams caster sugar

350 ml whole milk

olive oil, for the surface and proving bowl.

for the filling

300 grams dried mixed fruit

2 tsp ground cinnamon

75 grams light muscavado sugar

45 grams butter, melted

Directions

1. In a bowl add all the ingredients dough ingredients, keeping the yeast and salt apart. Combine all the ingredients with half of the milk.
2. Continue to mix, gradually adding more milk until fully combined.
3. Tip out onto a lightly oiled surface and knead for 10-15mins, until the dough becomes smooth.
4. Place the dough in a lightly oiled bowl and cover with cling film or tin foil and leave to prove for about 4hours.
5. Tip back out on a clean surface and knead for another 5mins.
6. Roll the dough out into a rectangular shape.
7. Paste over the melted butter. Follow this by sprinkling over the muscavado sugar, then the fruit and finish with the cinnamon.
8. Roll the dough (like you would a Swiss roll) tightly and portion out into 10 equal sized pieces. Leave to prove for 1 hour.
9. Pre-heat an oven to 220°C / 200°C fan.
10. Place the buns in the oven for 20mins. Reduce the heat to 190°C / 170°C fan and continue to bake for another 10mins.
11. Leave on a wire rack to cool.

Chocolate Chip Brioche

Ingredients

75 ml milk, tepid or room temperature

15 grams dried active yeast

500 grams strong white bread flour or plain flour

1 tbsp fine salt

6 medium eggs

350 grams butter, cubed at room temperature

30 grams caster sugar

1 egg yolk, beaten

100 grams chocolate chips

Directions

1. put the milk into a jug and whisk in the yeast.

2. Put the flour, salt and eggs into a bowl. Mix with your hands and then pour in the milk and yeast mix. Begin to knead the mix for about 2-3mins.

3. In a separate bowl, beat the butter and sugar together. Add a bit of the butter to the dough, knead the dough to combine the butter. Continue adding the butter bit by bit as you knead until you get an elasticy, amalgamated and glossy dough.

4. Cover the bowl with cling film and leave to stand at room temperature for 2 hours.

5. Beat down the dough, lift out of bowl and throw back into the bowl.. Do this a few times.

6. Recover the bowl and refrigerate for about 6 hours or more if you wish. Do not exceed 24 hours.

7. The dough is now ready to go split in half as the dough can make two loaves. Either freeze one or prepare two tins as follows.

8. Generously butter a loaf tin.

9. Pour some olive oil on the counter. Take the dough and flatten slightly with your hands.

10. Sprinkle over choc chips, fold and flatten slightly, fold again and repeat until all choc chips are added.

11. Place in the tin, cover and place in the fridge for 20-25mins.

12. Pre-heat an oven to 220°c / 200°c fan.

13. Brush the beaten yolk over the top of the dough.

14. Bake in oven for 10mins, reduce the heat to 190°c / 170°c fan. Bake for a further 25-30mins or until cooked through.

15. Remove and let stand for 5mins before removing from the tin.

Cinnamon and Mixed Fruit Bagels

Ingredients serves 6

500 grams stone ground wholemeal flour

15 grams dried active yeast

10 grams salt

1 tbsp ground cinnamon

4 tbsp olive oil

15 grams light muscavado sugar

350 ml water

100 grams mixed dried fruit

1 egg

Directions

1. Place all the dry ingredients (keep the mixed fruit to one side for later) and the oil into a bowl keeping the yeast away from the salt.
2. Pour in the water gradually until the dough begins to form. (You may not need it all)
3. Tip the dough onto a dry smooth surface and knead for 10mins.
4. Place the dough in a lightly oiled bowl and cover. Leave to prove for about 4hours.
5. Remove the dough and then knead for another 5mins. Gradually add the mixed fruit into the dough, during the kneading process, this will help the fruit be spread throughout the dough mixture.
6. Split into 6 equal sized balls, pierce the middle and swirl around your finger to create a ring shape. Place onto a baking tray lined with grease proof paper. (Make sure you leave room for the dough expanding, use a second tray if needed.)
7. Cover with a tea towel and prove for another 2hours.
8. Pre-heat an oven to 190°C / 170°C fan and bring a pan of water to boil.
9. One by one, boil each dough ring for 90s, turning over every 30s. Remove and place on a grease proof paper lined tray.
10. Crack the egg into a cup and beat with a fork. Use this to egg wash each bagel.
11. Place into the oven for 20-25mins or until golden brown.
12. Remove from the oven and allow to cool.

Ring Doughnuts

Ingredients serves 12

for the doughnut

500 grams strong white flour

300 ml milk, warmed up, do not boil

15 grams active dry yeast

10 grams salt

10 grams granulated sugar

20 grams unsalted butter

additional

100 grams granulated sugar

2 tbsp vegetable oil

2 tsp vanilla extract

Directions

1. In a bowl add all the doughnut ingredients, keeping the yeast and salt apart. Combine all the ingredients with half of the milk.
2. Continue to mix, gradually adding more milk until fully combined.
3. Tip out onto a lightly floured surface and knead for 10-15mins, until the dough becomes smooth.
4. Place the oil and vanilla extract in a large bowl. Mix together and the wipe it around the base and edges.
5. Place the dough in the bowl and cover with cling film or tin foil and leave to prove for about 4hours.
6. Tip back out on a clean surface and knead for another 5mins
7. Roll the dough into a long sausage shape and cut into even sized pieces.
8. Roll in each one into a ball. Punch a whole in the middle with you finger and then spin the dough around your finger to create a ring shape.
9. Heat oil in a large pot or in a deep fryer. Once it reaches around 160°C. Gently place the doughnut rings in using a metal slotted spoon.
10. Once one side is golden brown, turn them and cook on the other side.
11. Once both sides are golden in colour, remove and place on a plate with kitchen paper on. Repeat for all your doughnut rings.
12. Whilst still warm roll the rings in a bowl of caster sugar. Place to one side or eat.

Sesame Seed Bagels

500 grams strong white bread flour
15 grams dried active yeast
10 grams salt
15 grams light muscavado sugar
4 tbsp toasted sesame oil
350 ml water
1 egg
sesame seeds for topping

Directions

1. Place all the dry ingredients and the oil into a bowl keeping the yeast away from the salt.
2. Pour in the water gradually until the dough begins to form. (You may not need it all)
3. Tip the dough onto a dry smooth surface and knead for 10mins.
4. Place the dough in a lightly oiled bowl (with some more toasted sesame oil) and cover. Leave to prove for about 4hours.
5. Remove the dough and then knead for another 5mins.
6. Split into 8 equal sized balls, pierce the middle and swirl around your finger to create a ring shape. Place onto a baking tray lined with grease proof paper. (Make sure you leave room for the dough expanding, use a second tray if needed.)
7. Cover with a tea towel and prove for another 2hours.
8. Pre-heat an oven to 190°C / 170°C fan and bring a pan of water to boil.
9. One by one, boil each dough ring for 90s, turning over every 30s. Remove and place on a grease proof paper lined tray.
10. Crack the egg into a cup and beat with a fork. Use this to egg wash each bagel.
11. Sprinkle some sesame seeds over each bagel.
12. Place into the oven for 20-25mins or until golden brown.
13. Remove from the oven and allow to cool.

Sweets

& Treats

Chocolate Flapjack

Ingredients serves 27

325 grams rolled oats

400 grams light condensed milk

175 grams light brown muscavado sugar

180 grams butter

150 ml water

200 grams dessicated coconut

100 grams dark chocolate

25 grams white chocolate

4 tsp vanilla extract

Directions

1. Pre-heat an oven to 220°c / 200°c fan.
2. Add the butter, sugar, water, vanilla extract and condensed milk to a saucepan and heat on a medium heat.
3. Once the ingredients have created a nice toffee sauce, add in the coconut and stir in for 2-3mins.
4. Take off the heat and stir in the oats.
5. Pour onto a lined baking tray and spread evenly.
6. Place in the oven for 15-20mins or until browning on top.
7. Whilst your flap jack is cooking, melt the chocolate ready for spreading over the top.
8. Remove the flapjack and turn out onto a cooling rack. Be careful as it will be delicate.
9. Pour over the dark chocolate and spread evenly.
10. Using a spoon flick the white chocolate over the top to create a marbling effect.
11. Using a very sharp knife. Trim the edges and then cut into evenly sized pieces. You may need to occasionally wipe the knife as you go.
12. Leave to cool then place in the fridge.

Chocolate Coconut Pots

Ingredients serves 4

90 grams caster sugar

250 ml milk

3 egg yolks

1 tsp vanilla essence

2 tbsp cocoa powder (dark chocolate)

100 grams dessicated coconut

Directions

1. Place four ramekins on a baking tray and pouring some water until it reaches about half way. Pre-heat an oven to 145°c / 125°c fan.

2. Put the milk, 60g of sugar and essence into a pan and bring to boil on a medium heat.

3. Whisk the yolks and remaining sugar in a bowl, then add the cocoa powder and whisk some more.

4. Tip in the coconut and the gently pour some of the boiling milk in to the bowl, whisking constantly as you do it. Then add the contents back in to the pan of milk. Reduce the heat and stir until thickened. You will know it's ready when you can use your finger to create a line down the spoon and the mixture does not drip.

5. Spoon the mixture between the 4 ramekins and then place the oven for 20-25mins until firm to touch.

Chocolate Irish Cream Ice Cream

Ingredients

8 tbsp Irish Cream

300 ml Extra Thick Double Cream

300 ml Semi-skimmed Milk

125 grams Caster Sugar

1 tbsp Vanilla Extract

3 Egg Yolks

200 grams Dark Chocolate Drops

Directions

1. Cream the egg yolks and 25g of the sugar together in a heat proof bowl.
2. Place the milk, cream, vanilla extract and remaining sugar in a heavy based pan and bring to boil.
3. Pour a little of the heated milk over the egg yolks whisking as you do. Then pour the rest in.
4. Return the custard mix to the pan on a low heat and keep whisking.
5. Add 25g of the chocolate. Keep whisking the custard until thickened. (Good test - place a spoon in, pull out and use your finger to make a line on the back of spoon. If it does not fill in it's ready)
6. Once ready, tip out in to a heat and freezer proof tub, leaving to cool fully.
7. Once cooled, add the Irish cream and remaining chocolate drops.
8. Place the mixture in the freezer to set. Stir every 30-60mins to break down ice.

Coconut Ice Cream

50 grams dessicated coconut

200 ml coconut milk

175 ml condensed milk

175 ml double cream

1 tbsp ground almonds

1 tsp vanilla extract

1. Place all ingredients in a bowl and beat with a balloon whisk for 2-3mins.
2. Pour into a freezer friendly container and place in freezer until set. Check every two hours where possible, stirring with a fork to break down water crystals.

Mixed Flavour Flapjack Bites

Ingredients serves 24

425 grams rolled oats

400 grams condensed milk

175 grams light muscavado sugar

180 grams butter

150 ml water

4 tsp vanilla extract

100 grams dark chocolate

50 grams white chocolate

15 grams mixed fruit

1 lemon

15 tsp icing sugar

1 mandarin

Directions

1. Pre-heat an oven to 220°c / 200°c fan.
2. Line a mini muffin tin with grease proof paper or place in mini muffin cases.
3. Add the butter, sugar, water, vanilla extract and condensed milk to a saucepan and heat on a medium heat.
4. Once the ingredients have created a nice toffee sauce, take off the heat and stir into the oats.
5. Spoon in 2tsp's of the mixture into 15 of the muffin spaces.
6. In 3 separate bowls, spoon in 6tsp's of the mixture.
7. In one bowl, pour in the mixed fruit, mix with the flapjack mixture and then spoon 2tsp's into 3 of the muffin spaces.
8. In the next bowl, grate in the zest of the lemon. Cut the lemon in half, squeezing the juice of half the lemon into the bowl. Mix well and the spoon 2tsp's of the mixture into 3 of the muffin spaces.
9. In the final bowl, grate in half the zest of the mandarin. Cut the mandarin in half and squeeze the juice into the bowl. Mix well and then spoon 2tsp's of the mixture into 3 of the muffin spaces.
10. Place in the oven for 15-20mins or until browning on top.
11. Remove the flapjack and remove each flapjack, placing onto a wire rack to cool. Be careful as it will be delicate.
12. Once they have cooled, spoon 3tsp's of icing sugar into a bowl and squeeze in the juice of the other half of the lemon. Begin to mix, gradually adding more spoons of the icing sugar until all have been used.
13. Spoon this lemon icing on top of 3 of the 3 lemon infused flapjacks.
14. Melt the dark chocolate and spoon over 12 of the plain flapjacks and the 3 mandarin infused flapjacks.
15. Once the dark chocolate has set, melt the white chocolate and drip over the top of the 12 plain flapjacks with dark chocolate tops.
16. Once all of the flapjacks have cooled and set, you can now remove them from the cases/grease proof paper cases if you wish.

Nut Flapjack

Ingredients

250 grams rolled oats

50 grams dessicated coconut

50 grams sunflower seeds

150 grams hazelnuts, crushed into rough chunks

100 grams walnuts, crushed

75 grams whole almonds, crushed

150 grams dark chocolate drops

180 grams caster sugar

180 grams muscavado brown sugar

200 ml water

Directions

1. Mix together in a heat proof bowl the oats, coconut, walnuts, sunflower seeds, crushed almonds and chocolate drops

2. In a saucepan, heat the water and both sugars on a medium heat for about 10mins. Do not stir. It should reach about 104-105°c.

3. Add the hazelnut chunks to the pan for 2-3mins.

4. Take off the heat and mix into the bowl until combined thoroughly.

5. Tip the mixture into a baking tray lined with greaseproof paper and flatten down to desired thickness. Place the mixture in the fridge for 2-3 hours.

6. At this stage you can eat it if you like really sticky flapjack. Alternatively, pre-heat an oven to 220°c / 200°c fan.

7. Place the tray in the oven for 20-25mins or until browning on top. The mixture should become firmer and less sticky to touch.

8. Remove from oven, slice into pieces and allow to cool.

Oat Biscuits

Ingredients serves 12

115 grams butter

110 grams caster sugar

30 grams golden caster sugar

100 grams self raising flour

1 tbsp vanilla extract

140 grams rolled oats

1 tsp bicarbonate soda

2 tbsp semi skimmed milk

40 grams coco powder

Directions

1. Pre-heat an oven to 170°C / 150°C fan.
2. Cream together the butter, milk and sugar until light and fluffy.
3. Add the vanilla extract and mix in.
4. Beat in the bicarbonate soda.
5. Stir in the oats, coco and flour.
6. Using a desert spoon, take some of the mixture, roll into a ball, flatten and place on a tray.
7. Place in the oven and bake for 20-25 mins, until they are golden brown. Remove and allow to cool.

Panna Cotta

Ingredients serves 6

25 grams caster sugar

120 grams chocolate (50% cocoa)

280 ml double cream

280 ml milk

1 vanilla pod

3 gelatine

75 grams chocolate chips

Directions

1. Place the milk, double cream and sugar in a pan.
2. Split the vanilla pod, scrape out the seeds and place both the seeds and pod in the pan.
3. Place the gelatine leaves in cold water for 5mins.
4. Meanwhile, bring the pan to boil for 2-3mins.
5. Remove the pod and add the chocolate, whisking until the chocolate is melted.
6. Add the gelatine leaves and whisk until dissolved.
7. Remove from heat and pour the contents through a sieve into a bowl and leave to cool. Stir to prevent a skin.
8. Once cooled, ladle into ramekins and add the chocolate chips.
9. Place in the fridge for a minimum of 4 hours to set.

Red Berry Fudge Sorbet

Ingredients

180 ml water

85 grams raspberries

45 grams strawberries

200 ml whipping cream

1 tsp vanilla essence

8 ice cubes

200 grams caster sugar

Directions

1. Stir the cream, water and sugar together in a pan.

2. Place on a low heat stirring for 1-2mins.

3. Add the essence and berries and bring to boil on a medium heat.

4. Reduce heat and simmer until fruit breaks down.

5. Once the fruit has mostly broken down, use a masher to break up any larger pieces.

6. Tip into a heat resistance tub suitable for freezing, place in the freezer and stir every hour or so.

7. Serve once it's set but not solid. If it is too hard, allow to stand on the side until it loosens up.

Triple Chocolate Flapjack

Ingredients

250 grams unsalted butter

100 ml water

3 tsp vanilla extract

100 grams light muscavado sugar

5 tsp dark chocolate cocoa powder

315 grams rolled oats

200 grams dark chocolate

200 grams white chocolate

Directions

1. Pre-heat an oven to 220°C / 200°C fan.
2. In a heavy based pan, add the butter, sugar, water & vanilla extract. Gently heat together till fully melted and combined.
3. Take off the heat and add the oats. Mix well and then pour out into a baking tray. Place in the oven for 15-20mins.
4. Remove from the oven and all low to completely cool.
5. Once cooled, cut into slices. Begin to melt either the dark or white chocolate. Cover one side of the flap jack with the chocolate.
6. Allow the chocolate to set then repeat previous step.
7. Once set, place in the fridge to store.

INDEX

99

T

Lightning Source UK Ltd.
Milton Keynes UK
UKRC021340111019
351394UK00005B/118